YOUR KNOWLEDGE HAS VALUE

Bibliographic information published by the German National Library:

The German National Library lists this publication in the National Bibliography;
detailed bibliographic data are available on the Internet at http://dnb.dnb.de .

Imprint:

Copyright © 2016 GRIN Verlag, Open Publishing GmbH
Print and binding: Books on Demand GmbH, Norderstedt Germany
ISBN: 9783668276451

This book at GRIN:

http://www.grin.com/en/e-book/337925/the-divine-matrix-by-gregg-braden-a-book-
analysis

Christopher Mills

"The Divine Matrix" by Gregg Braden. A book analysis

GRIN Publishing

GRIN - Your knowledge has value

Since its foundation in 1998, GRIN has specialized in publishing academic texts by students, college teachers and other academics as e-book and printed book. The website www.grin.com is an ideal platform for presenting term papers, final papers, scientific essays, dissertations and specialist books.

Visit us on the internet:

http://www.grin.com/

http://www.facebook.com/grincom

http://www.twitter.com/grin_com

August 1, 2016

The Divine Matrix: Bridging Time, Space, Miracles & Belief by Gregg Braden

About the author

For more than 20 years, Braden has dedicated his energy as a spiritual seeker doing research and publishing five books. He has traveled throughout the world focusing on ancient and religious texts as well as served as a counselor for people seeking to mean in a spiritual context.

Introduction

Human beings exist in the world web of life with interconnections ultimately uniting nonbelievers and spiritual believers. In this case, non-believers are an important group since they insist on more solid proofs, which is the aim of this book. Most of them are unlike spiritual believers who accept faith without the need to reason. First, you have to be an admirer of science and religion to enjoy a great book that has had impacts on some people.

Book analysis

The Divine Matrix is an example of a link in the understanding of human beings according to research. Therefore the first step of tapping into this force is familiarizing ourselves with how it works and adopting a language best understood. For this reason, the author of The Divine Matrix: Bridging Time, Space, Miracles & Belief makes interesting revelations on how to discover and explores miracles in the Quantum world.

As the evidence suggests, most things in life begin from here such as healing, deep relationships, DNA of life and origin of the stars. Max Planck proposed the quantum theory in 1944 that promised to show the existence of Divine Matrix and the Universe within its containment. Synopsis of the argument begins during the era of Newtonian physics, through discoveries by Einstein to breakthroughs Braden proposed in the 21st Century. Explaining the holographic nature of man's observation in the quantum is possible through science a fact that Braden relates with quite well in his book.

However, until recently researchers discovered that it is indeed genuine, and authors like Braden present the concept as the first of twenty keys in The Divine Matrix: Bridging Time, Space, and Miracles & Belief, to explain how religion and science closely intertwine. In fact, the interesting belief is that the world created by us is an accurate reflection of beliefs, such that in order of finding inner peace, healing and obtaining happiness. Gregg Braden deserves credit for combining science, spirituality, and miracles in an interesting book using the language of Divine Matrix having put more than 20 years into research.

However, skeptics may speculate on some issues as much as the author's presentation of logic and convincing arguments, especially since the debate between religion and science, cannot be just resolved through a book. Alternatively, for those who read this book, the arguments about life are the interconnections in many unseen things in the universe and the potential of human beings to help build a more positive future.

Braden shares his findings in a book that can shift your paradigm using 20 keys of conscious creation able to assist the reader to translate miracles in imagination and putting it into practicality. Explained in basic science language easy to understand and written in the form of real life stories the author recognized that only our beliefs limit some of us, the result is a resourceful impact into our lives. For the benefit of this discussion, the 20 keys of conscious creation are highlighted to give a summary of Divine Matrix in the book.

The 20 keys of Divine Matrix by Braden Gregg

The first key states that Divine Matrix acts as the container which holds the universe, the bridge connecting all things, and the mirror that shows us what we have created. Therefore, our actions on one part of life have effects and influence the other parts. Braden describes Divine Matrix using three components mainly container, bridge, and mirror. Therefore, it holds the entire universe, acts as a connection between all things that exist, and shows what human beings have created. It is important to discuss the components of Divine Matrix to understand the language. Ideally, people live in small villages where both the effect of other people and how we affect them in a day. The global community felt and has significant weight. Accordingly, the relationships with people change the shape and nature of the universe. Therefore the role Divine Matrix plays is to act as a mirror that shapes people's beliefs and relationships.

A look at the concept of the bridge as earlier mentioned reveals an indication that the decisions people have to make while on Earth is narrowed down to the choice of living enjoyable and peacefully or making the same life boring or non-peaceful. Conflicts and warfare are because of creations of human beings and it is the same people who are instrumental in technological advancement that include exploration in the outer space. The concept realizes the fact that people may use facilities in right or wrong projects.

A mirror is a reflection of how individual behaviors affect other people in the society. Different relationships form the main component of a community and therefore are affected by relationships people have between each other. The concept of mirror advocates for responsibility for individual behavior and actions towards other people in the same society or different community. It is through the traditions and belief of a person that the whole communities' traditions and illuminated beliefs. Therefore; the individual is the mirror of the community and should seek to explain it.

Human beings should not look further because discoveries in the quantum world suggest that within each, there is something simply not limited by time, space and death instead the world we live in is nonlocal where everything connected to something. The claims strongly supported by Dean Radin, a senior scientist at the Institute of Noetic Sciences. Quantum field connects with everything and research proves to heal and obtain peace when we take our time to understand fully. Arguments by the author sensibly point to certain relevant facts and are a great discovery, which most people do not pay attention including mainstream media.

According to Gregg Braden, the second key in the Divine Matrix states how different things interconnected in the world. The proposal by the author says that Divine Matrix is holographic in that any portion of the quantum field contains everything else in the quantum field. Besides consciousness according to beliefs is holographic. For instance, prayers in our living room already exist with the people we love and where it is intended. According to these principles, prayers exists already where it belongs everywhere. Connections people have with each other will act as a facilitator of how people of one community respect and consider the individual behavior and beliefs of different communities. Moreover, it is the genesis of opportunities coming our way because we remain an integral part of that connectedness responsible for atoms, stars, and DNA.

People remain part of the universe the same way everything in the universe has a deeper connection to something else. Discovery made by the author is that none in the world both at individual and country levels has the capability to exist as an island away from other people since some vital roles need working together. Therefore, the connection with Divine Matrix makes it part of people's lives imposing them with the belief and action of either improving the world or make it worse. For this reason, the way to achieve this is by understanding how different conditions work, trying to know why we joined through connections and what they mean. It all begins with picturing ourselves differently possible by not separating ourselves from the world but instead becoming part of it.

Tapping force in the universe, it is important to look at ourselves in the context of the world rather than separating from every aspect of it; this is the third key of Divine Matrix. The implication is how the past, present, and future enjoin Divine Matrix being the container which holds time. In this case, connections are deep among everything that exists in the earth. Consequently, our choices are affected by continuity provided by the matrix. As the author breaks it down, everything that ever was and that which is yet to come has some deep connection with what is existing now. To achieve peace, abundance, healing, career, relationships, and experiences then connecting it to our reality is the sure way of finding joy. Scientific experiments point to origins of the ordinary world from the quantum field that is evenly spread in the universe and only recognized by people. Backed up with scientific knowledge shifting our thinking helps to tap power that lies in Divine Matrix.

The origin of the matrix attributed to an explosion of the universe that released massive energy by most scientists. The period 13 and 20 billion years ago, the small world exploded due to temperatures and created a pattern of energy still present to this day .The pattern of energy expands throughout the cosmos, connecting everything and its surroundings substantially forming the quantum field. Hence, Divine Matrix is created, acting as a multidimensional mirror, occasionally giving a reflection of emotions and beliefs in the world. Big bang theory explains how things are connected even though they appear so differently. In such an experiment conducted at the University of Geneva, single photons split into two identical twins a possible explanation for their connectivity. Conclusively, the same way photons and particles created show interconnection in everything whether the physical attachment exists or not.

Key number four according to the author states that things remain connected as long as they joined whether the bit is physically linked or not. At some point, the small universe, and everything physically joined only separated by the energy of the big bang. Readers will find this book read interesting but often relies upon scientific evidence to base claims.

Focusing on our consciousness is an act of creating and generating things states critical five. The quest to establish smallest particle and matter is futile in both the quantum world of atoms and the vast outer space only leaving conscienceless with the actual answer. Consciousness helps bring the dreams we have into reality and those imaginations to life so our ability to apply the understanding it shapes in our life and thinking. According to the author, Divine Matrix works with evidence that suggests power within our subconscious is the single field of energy human beings requires to incubate reality. Ultimately, this can lead to implications such as healing, war, peace or suffering. Perhaps the reminder is not to look at external vicissitudes in life that can result in the biggest error of how we view the universe.

The sixth key points out the power we need yet possess which enables us to create all changes we choose. Our capabilities depend on where our focus lies and in what ways we use the power of awareness the same way a difference exists between working towards a result and thinking or just feeling the desired effect. The author uses Neville's perspective to offer a better explanation from the book, Power of Awareness revealing that when people work towards achieving something the journey becomes open ended and never ending. Therefore identifying the goal and launching milestones to achieve it sets us on the right path rather than in the process of producing it that the mind has not yet registered. It starts with understanding possibilities to begin to realize our imaginations by fulfilling dreams and seeing our prayers answered. Understanding how quantum physics works overemphasized in this book since our world, our lives, and bodies somehow connect to these possibilities.

In the primary seven, when we focus on our awareness the result is the reality of our world. By now as enthusiasts of this book, you realize central to our question of our existence is our role in the universe. Apparently, it can be useful by trying to understand how scientific observations work in this field to apply it in our lives. For instance, double split experiment presents findings that sometimes the behavior of electrons goes according to our expectations same application to our daily life where we spate things and make others distinct.

Consciousness has a significant role in the universe helping us discover new adventures especially when electrons surprises in quantum. Divine Matrix plays an important role acting as the container of all observations hampered only by creating conscious conditions locking us from perceptions of reality. We have to look beyond illusions given by the world sometimes falling into pitfalls and learn the most valuable lesson that is the balance of choosing thoughts, feelings, and beliefs with a new possibility.

According to key, eight only selecting a new reality is not sufficient. Choice of a quantum potential dictated by assuming the way of being where focus locks out the possibility of flickering quantum solidifying our reality which is because of presence. Wisdom is no stranger to being found in the place where least expected since our feelings and emotions affect what reality made. Our secret language changes atoms, photons, and electrons of the world and don necessarily have to do with words people utter. Moreover, it speaks a language recognized by the Divine Matrix and where emotions speak to quantum forces within the universe.

Key number nine is about feeling a language that speaks to the Divine Matrix equated to the feeling of accomplishing our goals and prayers already answered. Foundations of the quantum principle tell us that feelings direct and focus our consciousness making it the easiest language Divine Matrix understands. However not every opinion applies to avoid confusions on how different people look at concepts and ideas overlap. Just like religious views of Buddhism, approaching a circumstance without expecting a wrong or right outcome helps achieve compassion, both a force of creation and experience that accesses it.

Proceeding without an ego or judgment is a sure way of going about it a quality of emotions is crucial to establishing an efficient and meaningful communication with the Divine Matrix. Every daily decision we involve ourselves in must not be approached with a hidden motive or based on egos. Therefore, to bring to bring the focus of our imagination, healing, belief, and peace, in reality, must be done in accordance without attaching the outcome of choice. Just like the interpretations of the Aramaic verses suggests, the invitation to prayer should be without judgment of what may happen or what should not occur.

Not just any feeling does it with the Divine Matrix, but one based on no experience and without ego is the tenth key stated by Braden Gregg. The principle based on the fact that people with stronger desires to change the world are elusive with power since they were driven by the ego probably offering an explanation to the reason why change is of so much significance to some people. Maturity into the state of consciousness alters our reality, and now this changes becomes less significant the same way our desire to drive a car wanes upon when we engage in that particular activity. Establishing an attachment with something that has not happened like in prayer has substantial implications on the outcome. It is the belief in reality exemplified by first believing, healing, finding abundance, believing in answers to prayers before it happens in our lives. Assumptions that these feelings last for short durations may make our reality a brief experience.

The eleventh key states that the things we choose to experience in our world reflected. The choice of feeling and what we are feeling at all times means we are always feeling. Convictions that peace exists somewhere in the world makes us grateful for peace in our life. Appreciating our well-being and those of our loved ones depends on the feeling of replenishment everyday reassign that if something exists in one location then definitely it will also exist somewhere else.

According to the twelfth key by Braden, the law of physics we know today does not bind us. For this reason, it starts with performing first the miracle and then it becoming available to everyone best experienced through the hologram. The holographic experience shows that things exist as a whole no matter the number of pieces divided. The idea conveyed is that each segment mirrors the entire universe no matter the division regarding human, atom, or galaxy.

In Key 13, a holographic object comprises of every piece that reflects the whole purpose. By definition, in a holographic piece, every place is a reflection of the entire object and properties displayed in one area exists elsewhere. The universe consists of a nonlocal hologram with properties of underlying energy linking all things instantly and establishing robust connections. The author gives evidence from scientists, and religious evidence eluded to such claims. So it points to the net that links everything together and within each point to reflect all the other points. Holographic qualities of the universe emanate from characteristics of a net where everything is visible to the others a techniques nature uses to survive, evolve, and grow. Each piece in the holographic universe mirrors the whole world in a small scale and everything for our survival and growth exists right here with us. In short, neither is anything is detached nor hidden within the Divine matrix.

According to key fourteen, the hologram universally connected with consciousness promises that the instant we create good wishes and prayers, they are already received at another destination. To put this into perspective, small changes in one part of the hologram changes everything reflected throughout the patterns. We are part of realities that exist within other realities, and our world is a projection of deeper things happening within us transforming those possibilities into realities. Everything we ever wish for is possible when we look at life from this perspective even transcending time and space.

The minimum number of people requires jumpstarting a change in consciousness is a squawroot of one percent of the population according to key sixteen. The act of watching through conscious observation is a window of possibilities of our reality carefully the mind choosing its expectations or the belief of what we have doing observation transmitting those into real experiences. Thus faith, belief or assumptions becomes the driving force in the quantum field and those who approach life from a point of view that horrible suffering or most joyous ecstasy are all possibilities find inner peace in themselves. The secret is bringing that power into intervening realities and imagining, dreaming and believing silently.

Key seventeenth says Divine Matrix serves as the mirror in our world of relationships created in our beliefs. We live in a world always reflecting our lives in deeper ideas, emotions rushing from events in life, while the everyday world reminds us of the deeper feelings within us. What our true convictions are, love and fears are shown through the personal mirror often the world acting as a literal mirror with too much to face for ourselves. Window created is a direct glimpse into reality within dreams we hold sometimes resulting into reflections coming in unexpected ways.

According to Braden Gregg, the eighteenth key indicates the origin of our negative experiences reduced to one of three fears in the universe namely: abandonment, lack of trust and low self-worth. The change came when the matrix offered the chance to outshine deceptive thoughts avoiding conflicts from within inner beliefs and outer world. For the benefit of our security in the world, we have to trust typically lessons learned from life experiences.

Our true beliefs are mirrored based on the most intimate relationship as stated in core nineteen to mean that Divine Matrix acts as a surface that is neutral to the reflections projected onto it. Recognizing judgments through relationships reverberate through the soul of human beings and everyone in our lives deserves appreciation because they show us an absolute reflection of life. Ability to bless things that have had an adverse impact on our lives suspends the cycle of pain temporarily since it is the only feeling that can replace another sense. Also, no amount of time in postponing the pain makes any difference as an opportunity soon rises to relinquish our healing and move on with life.

The last key in the book explores what we must become in our lives the very things we choose to experience in the world we live. Within the mode of seeing ourselves those things, we consider impossible come into reality. It is all in the imaginations realized each time we communicate using a language understood by our inner selves expressing a feeling, prayer or belief translated into our daily lives.

Conclusion

In conclusion, human beings can call it whatever, science, fiction, or religion but according to Braden, the truth is clearly, something is out there in the quantum field. Force, or presence with immense powers linking us with one another in the universe. Adopting these 20 fundamental principles gives life a new meaning when grasped as they contain invaluable lessons about relationships with each other and universe. The transformation we can undergo is that of a participant rather than a victim of unknown and unseen forces from where empowerment begins in our lives. Through unexpected experiences, quantum particles operate beyond time, peace and a miracle, therefore, doing the impossible requires pushing beyond what previously they thought was true. Realizing miracles in our lives comes from overcoming beliefs in phenomena that are impossible.

Work cited:

Braden, Gregg. The Divine Matrix. Carlsbad, Calif.: Hay House, 2007. Print.